The News Detox Prescription

Restoring Health in a World of Negativity.

Copyright Notice

Disclaimer

The information provided in this book, "The News Detox Prescription: Restoring Health in a World of Negativity," is intended for general informational purposes only. While every effort has been made to ensure the accuracy and completeness of the information presented, the author and publisher assume no responsibility for errors or omissions, or for any results obtained from the use of the information contained in this book. Readers are encouraged to exercise their own judgment and seek professional advice if needed.

Contents

Introduction

In a world saturated with a constant stream of information, we find ourselves bombarded by a barrage of news, much of it filled with negativity, chaos, and despair.

The 24-hour news cycle, social media platforms, and sensational headlines have become an inescapable part of our daily lives, shaping our thoughts, emotions, and even our well-being.

As we navigate through the digital landscape, it becomes increasingly clear that our mental and emotional health is at stake.

"The News Detox Prescription: Restoring Health in a World of Negativity" invites you to embark on a transformative journey towards reclaiming your inner peace in the midst of a turbulent information age.

In these pages, we will explore the impact of constant exposure to negative news on our mental, emotional, and physical well-being.

More importantly, we will unveil a holistic approach to detoxifying ourselves from the relentless onslaught of pessimism and restoring balance to our lives.

This book is not a call to ignorance or a dismissal of the importance of staying informed.

Instead, it is a guide to cultivating a mindful and intentional relationship with the news—a prescription for a healthier media consumption that nourishes your mind, uplifts your spirit, and contributes to the overall well-being of both individuals and society.

As we navigate the terrain of this News Detox Prescription, you will discover the mind-body connection and how it relates to negative news consumption.

Together, we will explore crafting a personal news diet, delve into the social implications of individual news consumption habits, and address news literacy in our modern age.

Join me on this journey towards a healthier and more balanced relationship with the news.

Let's step away from the relentless negativity, rediscover the joy in our lives, and create a space for optimism and resilience to flourish.

Chapter 1

The Overdose Epidemic

In the relentless tide of news inundating our lives, one harrowing crisis that has taken center stage is the overdose epidemic.

As communities grapple with the devastating consequences of substance abuse, the pervasive coverage of this epidemic has become a constant presence, shaping public perception and fueling concerns.

Beyond the headlines and statistics, this chapter delves into the cost of information overload and the impact of incessant news consumption, shedding light on the toll it takes on individuals navigating the tumultuous currents of this public health crisis.

The Hidden Costs of Living in an Age of Information Overload

Living in an age of information overload comes with hidden costs that can impact various aspects of individual and societal well-being:

1 **Cognitive Overload:** Constant exposure to vast amounts of information can overwhelm cognitive resources, leading to difficulty in processing and retaining important details.

Even decision-making can be impaired when one is bombarded with too many choices or conflicting information.

2 **Reduced Attention Span:** Information overload contributes to a shortened attention span as individuals become accustomed to quickly scanning and consuming information.

This can hinder deep, focused thinking and the ability to engage in sustained, meaningful activities.

3 **Decreased Productivity:** Information overload can lead to multitasking and constant task-switching, which has been shown to decrease overall productivity.

Individuals may struggle to prioritize tasks and manage time effectively in the face of an overwhelming amount of information.

4 **Quality of Information:** The sheer volume of information can make it challenging to discern between credible and unreliable sources.
Misinformation and disinformation can spread easily, leading to misguided decisions and beliefs.

5 **Social Isolation:** Despite the interconnectedness facilitated by technology, information overload can contribute to social isolation as individuals may retreat into digital bubbles or disengage from real-life interactions.

Constant connectivity to devices may reduce the quality of face-to-face relationships.

6 **Health Impacts:** Information overload, particularly when related to stress-inducing or negative content, can contribute to mental health issues such as anxiety and depression.
Sleep disorders may arise from excessive screen time and exposure to information, especially before bedtime.

7 **Loss of Privacy:** In an information-rich environment, personal data is constantly collected, shared, and analyzed.
Individuals may experience a loss of privacy as their online activities, preferences, and personal information

are tracked and exploited for various purposes.

8 **Erosion of Critical Thinking:** The constant stream of information, especially through social media, can contribute to echo chambers and filter bubbles, limiting exposure to diverse perspectives.

Critical thinking skills may erode as individuals are less exposed to challenging viewpoints and nuanced discussions.

9 **Environmental Impact:** The production, storage, and transmission of vast amounts of digital information contribute to the environmental impact of data centers and electronic devices.

E-waste disposal and energy consumption associated with data processing contribute to environmental degradation.

10 **Economic Costs:** The time spent on information consumption, often in the form of social media or online news, can lead to decreased productivity in the workplace.

Addiction to information consumption may lead to reduced focus on work tasks, impacting overall economic productivity.

Impact of Constant News Consumption on Mental and Emotional Well-Being

Constant news consumption can have a significant and pervasive impact on mental and emotional well-being.

While staying informed is important, the way news is presented, the frequency of updates, and the nature of the content can contribute to various challenges:

1 **Anxiety and Stress:** Continuous exposure to negative news, especially concerning events like natural disasters, conflicts, or crises, can lead to heightened anxiety and stress.

Sensationalized or alarmist headlines creates a sense of urgency and fear, contributing to a constant state of alertness.

2 **Information Overload:** The constant influx of news from various sources can lead to information overload, making it challenging for individuals to process and prioritize information.

Overconsumption of news may result in cognitive fatigue, difficulty concentrating, and a feeling of being overwhelmed.

3 **Desensitization:** Repeated exposure to distressing news can lead to desensitization, where individuals become emotionally numb or indifferent to subsequent events.

This desensitization can impact empathy and the ability to connect emotionally with others who may be experiencing distress.

4 **Confirmation Bias and Polarization:** Continuous exposure to news from specific sources can reinforce existing beliefs and contribute to confirmation bias.

The polarized nature of news reporting can further divide society, leading to increased tension and a sense of 'us versus them.'

5 **Social Comparison and Fear of Missing Out (FOMO):** Constant exposure to others' achievements, experiences, or reactions through news and social media can foster social comparison and feelings of inadequacy.

Fear of missing out on important information or events can lead to compulsive news-checking behavior, contributing to stress and anxiety.

6 **Sleep Disruption:** Late-night news consumption, especially if it involves distressing or anxiety-inducing content, can contribute to sleep disturbances. Lack of quality sleep can, in turn, negatively impact overall mental and emotional well-being.

7 **Loss of Perspective:** Focusing excessively on negative news may lead to a skewed perception of reality, overlooking positive developments and fostering a sense of hopelessness.

8 **Impact on Relationships:** Constant discussions about distressing news topics can strain interpersonal relationships, especially when individuals have differing opinions.

Emotional fatigue and heightened sensitivities may contribute to conflicts within families, workplaces, or communities.

Signs of News Addiction

Here are some signs that may indicates that you are struggling with news addiction:

1 **Constant Checking:** You are struggling with news addiction, if you notice a compulsive urge to check for updates

regularly, sometimes multiple times a day.

This may be because you feel an intense need to stay informed at all times, sometimes prioritizing this over other responsibilities or activities.

2 **Inability to Disconnect:** You struggle to detach from news sources, whether it's social media or news apps, even during your downtime.

The thought of being disconnected from the latest updates makes you feel uneasy and restless.

It's challenging to relax when you're not in the loop, and the constant need to stay updated keeps you glued to your devices, even during personal moments.

3 **Increased Consumption During Stressful Events:** During times of increased stress or anxiety, your news consumption intensifies, feeding into a cycle of emotional distress.

You find yourself checking the news more frequently, especially during crises or significant events, seeking reassurance or information.

However, this heightened exposure to news exacerbates your feelings of unease, perpetuating the cycle of anxiety.

4 **Neglect of Responsibilities:** You find yourself neglecting daily responsibilities, work, and social activities because your attention is consumed by the constant stream of news.

It's hard to concentrate on anything else; your mind is always fixated on the latest headlines. Tasks that used to be simple now feel daunting as your focus wavers, drifting back to the news.

You may also struggle to maintain attention in non-news-related contexts, feeling restless and anxious when not plugged into updates.

5 **Emotional Distress:** You find yourself grappling with intense emotional turmoil, triggered by the news you consume.

Anxiety grips you tightly, and fear becomes a constant companion as you navigate through the onslaught of information.

Each news story seems to wield power over your emotions, leaving you struggling to maintain stability.

Managing your reactions becomes a daunting task, as mood swings become more frequent, and negativity seeps into every corner of your mind.

Despite your efforts, the weight of the news persists, casting a shadow over your well-being.

6 **Insomnia or Sleep Disturbances:** Before hitting the sack, you find yourself endlessly scrolling through news updates, unable to resist the urge to check for the latest headlines.

This habit wreaks havoc on your sleep routine, making it tough to drift off or causing frequent awakenings throughout the night.

Exposure to distressing or overly stimulating news stories further compounds the issue, leaving your mind buzzing with worry or excitement when it should be winding down for rest.

The compulsive need to stay informed may be robbing you of precious sleep, impacting your overall well-being and leaving you feeling drained and unrested come morning.

7 **Physical Symptoms:** You might experience physical symptoms like headaches, eye strain, and fatigue from extended screen time and constant news consumption.

You may begin to neglect self-care activities, such as exercise and healthy eating, as a consequence of being overly absorbed in the news cycle.

8 **Social Isolation:** You find yourself withdrawing from social interactions, opting instead to immerse in consuming news.

Conversations and activities unrelated to current events seem difficult to engage in. Your focus narrows to the latest headlines, discussions revolving around news topics becoming your primary interest.

Friends may notice your shift, perhaps feeling disconnected as your conversations lean heavily on what's happening in the world.

9 **Polarization and Aggressive Behavior:** You often find yourself drawn into heated debates or arguments with others, particularly online, triggered by strong emotional reactions to news stories.

There's a tendency to adopt extreme viewpoints and exhibit aggressive behavior during these discussions.

Sometimes, the intensity of your emotions can overshadow the opportunity for constructive dialogue, leading to confrontations rather than understanding.

10 **Compulsive Sharing:** Another sign of news addiction is that you feel a

compulsive need to constantly share news updates on social media or with friends and family.

It's as if there's an itch you must scratch, a relentless drive to disseminate the latest information.

This behavior isn't merely about staying informed; it's about seeking validation or a sense of purpose through the act of sharing news. Each share, each like or comment, reaffirms your connection to the world and your role within it.

The Need for News Detox

News detox involves intentionally taking a break from news consumption to restore balance, protect mental well-being, and foster a healthier relationship with information.

In today's age of constant information flow, news detox is a crucial step in mitigating the negative effects of news overload.

Here are some reasons why news detox is necessary:

1 **Reducing Information Overload:** News detox helps you break free from the constant stream of information, reducing cognitive overload and allowing the mind to rest.

It provides an opportunity to step back and evaluate the impact of information consumption on your mental and emotional well-being.

2 **Managing Anxiety and Stress:** Taking a break from news helps to alleviate anxiety and stress associated with distressing or negative news content.

It allows you to focus on your immediate surroundings and personal life without being constantly exposed to potentially upsetting information.

3 **Promoting Mental Health:** A news detox is a proactive approach to safeguarding your mental health. It allows for a reset, giving you the chance to prioritize self-care and engage in activities that bring joy and relaxation.

It can contribute to improved sleep patterns, reduced emotional fatigue, and a more positive outlook.

4 **Breaking the Addiction Cycle:** A news detox helps break the cycle of compulsive news checking and constant connectivity. It encourages you to develop a healthier relationship with information consumption, emphasizing quality over quantity.

5 **Gaining Perspective:** Stepping away from news allows you to gain perspective on the broader aspects of life.

It helps in recognizing that not every piece of information is urgent or requires immediate attention, fostering a sense of control and mindfulness.

6 **Encouraging Critical Reflection:** During a news detox, you reflect on your news consumption habits, identifying sources

of stress and evaluating the impact of different types of news on your well-being.

It provides an opportunity to reassess the need for constant connectivity and make informed decisions about future news consumption.

7 **Reconnecting with Real-Life Interactions:** A news detox encourages you to focus on face-to-face interactions, fostering stronger connections with friends, family, and the local community.

It helps in rediscovering the richness of personal relationships and experiences beyond the digital realm.

8 **Setting Healthy Boundaries:** Implementing regular news detox

periods allows you to establish healthy boundaries for information consumption. It empowers you to control when, where, and how you engage with news, preventing it from dominating you.

9 **Improving Productivity:** By taking a break from news, you'd experience improved focus and productivity in your work and daily activities.

It allows for a more intentional use of time, with less distraction and greater efficiency.

10 **Developing Sustainable Habits:** A news detox is not just a temporary break but an opportunity to develop sustainable and mindful news consumption habits.

It encourages you to be more selective about the sources and types of news you engage with, promoting a balanced approach.

Chapter 2

The Mind-Body Connection

Central to The News Detox Prescription is the profound recognition of the intricate interplay between mind and body, encapsulated within the concept of "The Mind-Body Connection."

In an era dominated by the constant barrage of negative news, the toll on mental health manifests physically, intertwining the well-being of the mind and body.

The Mind-Body Connection underscores the understanding that mental and emotional states significantly impact physical health, and vice versa.

As individuals grapple with the weight of distressing news, particularly concerning issues like the overdose epidemic, this facet of the prescription becomes an essential guide towards restoring equilibrium in a world rife with negativity.

By delving into The Mind-Body Connection, The News Detox Prescription encourages a holistic approach to well-being, recognizing that mental health is not isolated from physical health.

Chronic stress, anxiety, and emotional exhaustion resulting from constant exposure to negative news can manifest as physical symptoms, contributing to a cycle of deteriorating health.

Through mindful practices, stress reduction techniques, and fostering positive mental states, individuals can break free from the detrimental loop of negativity, promoting a harmonious balance between mind and body.

The Relationship between Mental Health and Physical Well-Being

The relationship between mental health and physical well-being is a well-established aspect of overall wellness.

Let's explore this relationship in more detail:

1 **Stress Response:**

Mental Health: Continuous exposure to negative news can trigger stress, anxiety, and even depression. The human mind tends to focus on threatening information, which can lead to a heightened state of alertness and persistent worry.

Physical Well-being: Chronic stress is linked to various physical health issues such as cardiovascular problems, weakened immune system, and digestive disorders. The body's stress response, when activated frequently, can have detrimental effects on overall health.

2 **Cognitive Function:**

Mental Health: Negative news overload may impair cognitive function, affecting decision-making, problem-solving, and memory. It can lead to a pessimistic outlook on life.

Physical Well-being: Cognitive function is closely tied to physical health. Impaired cognitive abilities can impact lifestyle choices, including diet, exercise, and sleep patterns, thereby influencing physical well-being.

3 **Sleep Patterns:**

Mental Health: Constant exposure to distressing news can contribute to sleep disturbances, insomnia, and nightmares.

Physical Well-being: Quality sleep is crucial for physical health and overall well-being. Lack of proper sleep is associated with various health issues, including obesity, diabetes, and compromised immune function.

4 **Behavioral Patterns:**

Mental Health: Negative news can influence behavioral patterns, leading to avoidance, social withdrawal, or heightened aggression.

Physical Well-being: Social connections and engagement are crucial for physical health. Isolation and negative behavior patterns can contribute to a decline in physical well-being.

5 **Hormonal Imbalance:**

Mental Health: Prolonged exposure to stress, often triggered by negative news, can disrupt hormonal balance, leading to issues like increased cortisol levels.

Physical Well-being: Hormonal imbalance can contribute to various physical health problems, including metabolic disorders, weight gain, and reproductive issues.

6 **Coping Mechanisms:**

Mental Health: Constant exposure to negativity can challenge coping mechanisms, leading to unhealthy responses such as substance abuse or emotional eating.

Physical Well-being: Unhealthy coping mechanisms can directly impact physical health, contributing to issues like addiction, obesity, and related health complications.

Chapter 3

The Science Behind the Headlines

The allure of news headlines is undeniable—they grab our attention, pique our curiosity, and often shape our perceptions of the world around us.

Yet, behind their seemingly innocuous façade lies a complex interplay of psychology, neuroscience, and media dynamics.

Understanding the science behind how news headlines impact us unveils a fascinating realm where cognitive processes, emotional responses, and societal influences converge.

From evoking visceral reactions to shaping our worldview, the power of headlines to influence our thoughts, emotions, and behaviors is profound.

In this chapter, we'll delve into the mechanisms through which news headlines exert their influence, shedding light on the relationship between media consumption and the human psyche.

The Mechanism of News Influence

News headlines exert influence through various psychological and cognitive mechanisms that capture attention, shape perceptions, and drive behaviors.

Here are some of the key ways headlines exert their influence:

1 **Attention Capture:** Headlines are designed to grab attention quickly. They often use compelling language, provocative statements, or emotional triggers to pique curiosity and encourage readers to click or engage with the content.

2 **Priming:** Headlines can prime readers' minds, influencing how they interpret subsequent information in the article.

For example, a sensationalist headline may prime readers to expect a dramatic or alarming story, shaping their perception of the content before they even begin reading.

3 **Emotional Response:** Effective headlines evoke emotional responses such as curiosity, fear, anger, or empathy. Emotions play a significant role in decision-making and memory formation, so headlines that trigger strong emotional reactions are more likely to be remembered and shared.

4 **Social Proof:** Headlines that imply urgency or importance can create a sense of social proof, making readers feel compelled to click or share in order to stay informed or appear knowledgeable to others in their social networks.

5 **Saliency and Framing:** The way a headline frames an issue can influence how it is perceived and understood.

By highlighting certain aspects of a story while downplaying others, headlines can shape the narrative and influence readers' opinions on a particular topic.

6 **Curiosity Gap:** Headlines create a "curiosity gap" by providing enough information to spark interest but leaving some questions unanswered.
This motivates readers to click through to the full article in search of answers.

Headlines play a crucial role in capturing attention and enticing readers to click on articles, but they can also have unintended side effects, contributing to mindless scrolling on the internet.

Here are some potential side effects:

1 **Clickbaiting**: Sensational or misleading headlines designed solely to generate clicks can lead to disappointment when the content fails to deliver on the promise of the headline.

This can contribute to a habit of mindlessly scrolling to find content that does deliver.

2 **Distractibility**: Catchy or provocative headlines can distract individuals from their intended tasks, leading to a cycle of aimless scrolling as they hop from one headline to the next without a clear purpose or objective.

3 **Emotional Manipulation**: Headlines that evoke strong emotions such as fear, outrage, or curiosity can trigger impulsive

reactions, prompting individuals to click on articles without fully considering the implications or validity of the information presented.

4 **FOMO (Fear of Missing Out):** Headlines that promise exclusive or time-sensitive information can trigger FOMO, compelling individuals to click on articles out of a fear of missing out on something important or valuable.

How News Consumption Affects the Brain

Several psychological studies and neuroscience research have delved into understanding how news consumption affects the brain. Here are some key findings from relevant studies:

1 **Negativity Bias:**

Research: Psychological studies, such as those conducted by psychologists like Roy Baumeister, have shown that humans have a negativity bias.

This means that negative information tends to have a more significant impact on the brain than positive information. Evolutionarily, this bias likely developed as a survival mechanism, where being attuned to potential threats or dangers in the environment was crucial for ensuring survival.

As a result, negative stimuli tend to elicit stronger emotional responses and are more readily remembered than positive stimuli.

This bias can influence various aspects of human cognition and behavior, including decision-making, risk assessment, and media consumption.

Neuroscience: Neuroscientific research using techniques like functional magnetic resonance imaging (fMRI) has demonstrated that the brain responds more strongly to negative stimuli.

The amygdala, a region associated with emotional processing, tends to be particularly activated in response to negative news.

2 **Stress Response and Cortisol Levels:**

Research: A study published in the journal "Psychoneuroendocrinology" found that exposure to negative news increased participants' stress levels, as measured by cortisol levels.

Neuroscience: Neuroscientific studies have demonstrated that chronic stress, triggered by negative news exposure, can lead to alterations in the brain's structure and function, affecting areas such as the hippocampus and prefrontal cortex.

3 **Fear and Anxiety:**

Research: Studies, including research by Graham Davey, a professor of psychology, have explored how exposure to negative news can contribute to heightened fear and anxiety levels.

Neuroscience: Functional brain imaging studies have identified neural circuits associated with fear and anxiety responses, showing increased activity in regions like the amygdala and the anterior cingulate cortex in response to threatening information.

4 Impact on Memory and Cognitive Function:

Research: Psychological research has highlighted the impact of emotional arousal on memory consolidation. It showed that negative news tends to be more memorable.

Neuroscience: Neuroimaging studies have revealed that emotional arousal, whether positive or negative, can modulate activity in the hippocampus and other memory-related brain regions.

5 Dopamine Release and Novelty:

Research: The role of dopamine in news consumption has been explored in studies investigating the brain's response to novel or unexpected information.

The result indicated that there is a dopamine release during the consumption of news which is associated with reward and motivation.

This is probably why we keep coming back to check news updates. We want more dopamine.

Neuroscience: Neuroscientific studies using fMRI and positron emission tomography (PET) scans have shown increased dopamine release in response to novel or surprising news, indicating the brain's reward system involvement.

Chapter 4

Crafting a Personal News Diet

In the pursuit of restoring mental health amid the overwhelming negativity in today's news landscape, "Crafting a Personal News Diet" emerges as a crucial component of "The News Detox Prescription."

This concept emphasizes the need for you to take an active and intentional role in curating the sources and types of news you consume.

Crafting a Personal News Diet involves a thoughtful selection of information outlets, focusing on credibility, diversity, and reliability.

By being discerning about the content and frequency of news consumption, you can tailor your news intake to align with your well-being goals, reducing the potential negative impact on mental health.

This proactive approach recognizes that not all news is created equal, and you have the agency to shape your media environment.

The idea of Crafting a Personal News Diet within the context of "The News Detox Prescription" is grounded in the understanding that information overload and constant exposure to distressing news can contribute to stress and anxiety.

By adopting a personalized and mindful approach to news consumption, you strike a balance between staying informed and safeguarding your mental health.

This strategy encourages individuals to prioritize quality over quantity, fostering a more intentional and empowered relationship with the news.

Crafting a Personal News Diet aligns with the broader goal of the News Detox Prescription, providing a practical framework for you to regain control over your information intake and promote a healthier mental and emotional state.

Developing a Personalized Approach to News Consumption

Developing a personalized approach to news consumption involves mindful consideration of your preferences, values, and mental well-being.

Here's a guide to help you tailor your news consumption habits to create a more balanced and positive experience:

1 **Reflect on Personal Values and Interests:** Start by reflecting on personal values and interests. Consider the topics and issues that matter most to you.

Ask yourself: What are my priorities, and what kind of information aligns with my values?

2 **Identify Trusted and Balanced Sources:** Identify a few reliable and balanced news sources that align with your values. Consider sources known for unbiased reporting and fact-checking.

Diversify your sources to get a well-rounded perspective on current events.

3 **Set Specific Time Limits:** Establish specific time limits for daily news consumption. Decide how much time you want to dedicate to staying informed without feeling overwhelmed.

Consider using tools or apps that limit your daily news intake to avoid mindless scrolling.

4 **Choose the Right Platforms:** Select news platforms that match your preferred

communication style. Whether you prefer reading articles, watching videos, or listening to podcasts, choose platforms that resonate with your preferences.

Opt for platforms that offer positive and solution-focused content in addition to news updates.

5 **Curate Your News Feed:** Customize your news feed to focus on topics of interest. Unfollow or mute sources that consistently contribute to a negative or stressful experience.

Use customization features on social media platforms to filter and prioritize content that aligns with your preferences.

6 **Schedule News Consumption Mindfully:** Schedule specific times for news consumption to avoid constant exposure throughout the day. Choose moments when you can give your full attention to the information.

Avoid checking the news right before bedtime to promote better sleep hygiene.

7 **Balance Negative News with Positive Content:** Actively seek out positive and uplifting news content to balance the impact of negative stories. Include sources that highlight solutions, human achievements, and inspiring stories.

Create a playlist or bookmark positive news websites to integrate into your daily routine.

8 **Engage in Offline Activities:** Balance your digital news consumption with offline activities. Spend time engaging in hobbies, physical exercise, or spending quality time with loved ones.

Consider designating specific days for a complete break from online news.

9 **Stay Informed Without Overconsumption:** Stay informed without becoming overwhelmed by focusing on the most relevant and impactful news for your life. Prioritize quality over quantity in your news consumption.

Consider subscribing to newsletters or using news aggregator apps that provide curated and summarized content.

10 **Practice Digital Detox:** Regularly practice digital detox to create mental space and reduce the impact of constant information overload. Designate certain days or weekends for a complete break from digital devices.

Use this time to connect with nature, practice mindfulness, or engage in activities that promote mental well-being.

11 **Regularly Assess and Adjust:** Periodically assess your news consumption habits. Evaluate how they align with your well-being and adjust your approach accordingly.

Be open to modifying your personalized news consumption plan as your preferences and priorities evolve.

Tips on Selecting Reliable News Sources

Selecting reliable sources is crucial for staying well-informed and avoiding misinformation. Here are some tips to help you identify and choose reliable sources for news consumption:

1 **Check the Source's Reputation:** Look for well-established and reputable news organizations with a history of unbiased reporting.

Verify the credibility of the source by researching its reputation, awards, and any potential controversies.

2 **Verify the Author's Credentials:** Check the author's qualifications and expertise in the subject matter.

Authors with relevant experience, education, or expertise are more likely to provide accurate and well-informed perspectives.

3 **Diversify Your Sources:** Avoid relying solely on one news source. Diversify your information intake by consulting multiple sources, which can provide a more comprehensive and balanced view of an issue.

Compare how different sources cover the same news to identify potential biases.

4 **Examine the Publication's Editorial Standards:** Investigate the publication's editorial standards and fact-checking processes. Reputable news outlets have clear guidelines for accuracy and fairness. Check if the publication corrects errors transparently and promptly.

5 **Evaluate the Use of Anonymous Sources:** Be cautious when a news article heavily relies on anonymous sources. Reputable sources use anonymity sparingly and provide context for why sources are not named.

Consider the credibility of the publication and the journalist in such cases.

6 **Consider the Tone and Objectivity:** Assess the tone of the news source.

Reliable news articles maintain objectivity, presenting facts without excessive sensationalism or emotional language.

Be wary of sources that exhibit a clear bias or use inflammatory language.

7 **Check for Citations and References:** Reliable articles include citations and references to support claims and provide additional context.

Cross-reference information by checking the cited sources to ensure accuracy.

8 **Be Skeptical of Clickbait and Sensational Headlines:** Avoid sources that rely on clickbait or sensationalized headlines to attract attention. Reliable news outlets prioritize accuracy over sensationalism.

Read beyond the headlines to understand the full context of the story.

9 **Assess the Timeliness of the Information:** Check for the publication date of the news article. Timeliness is crucial to ensure the information is current and relevant.

Be cautious of outdated information or news that may have evolved since the original report.

10 **Use Fact-Checking Websites:** Utilize fact-checking websites to verify the accuracy of information. Fact-checkers assess claims made in news articles and rate their accuracy.

Common fact-checking websites include Snopes, FactCheck.org, and PolitiFact.

11 **Beware of Biased Reporting:** Identify any potential biases in the reporting. Consider the overall political stance or affiliations of the news outlet.

Balance your news intake by consulting sources with different perspectives to gain a more comprehensive understanding.

12 **Seek Out Investigative Journalism:** Support news outlets that invest in investigative journalism. In-depth reporting often uncovers crucial details and provides a more thorough analysis of complex issues.

Recognize and appreciate the value of well-researched and comprehensive reporting.

Chapter 5

Nurturing Positivity

In the face of a media landscape often saturated with negative news, "Nurturing Positivity" advocates for intentional efforts to foster a more positive and balanced mental state.

Recognizing the profound impact that continuous exposure to distressing headlines can have on one's well-being, "Nurturing Positivity" encourages individuals to seek out uplifting and constructive news sources.

By consciously integrating positive news stories into your media consumption, you can counteract the pervasive negativity and cultivate a more optimistic and resilient mindset.

Within the context of "The News Detox Prescription," "Nurturing Positivity" aligns with the overarching goal of restoring mental health by emphasizing the transformative power of positive information.

This approach is not about ignoring the challenges and issues present in the world but rather about achieving a more balanced perspective.

By intentionally incorporating positive narratives into your news diet, you can create a psychological buffer against the detrimental effects of constant exposure to negative news.

The importance of positive news and uplifting stories.

The importance of positive news and uplifting stories goes beyond mere feel-good moments; it plays a crucial role in shaping our perceptions, mental well-being, and societal outlook.

Here are several reasons highlighting the significance of positive news:

1 **Positive Impact:** Positive news stories contribute to improved mental well-being by evoking positive emotions, such as joy, hope, and inspiration.

2 **Counterbalance to Negativity:** Constant exposure to negative news can lead to

stress, anxiety, and a sense of helplessness. Positive news serves as a counterbalance, promoting emotional balance and resilience.

3 **Stress Reduction:** Positive news has been linked to reduced stress levels. It provides a respite from the often distressing and anxiety-inducing content prevalent in mainstream news.

4 **Promotes Emotional Health:** Uplifting stories can enhance overall emotional health, leading to a more positive and optimistic outlook on life.

5 **Source of Inspiration:** Positive news and uplifting stories inspire and motivate individuals by showcasing the resilience, kindness, and achievements of people.

They highlight the potential for positive change.

6 **Encourages Positive Action:** Inspirational stories can spur individuals to take positive actions, whether in their personal lives or by contributing to community and global initiatives.

7 **Promotes Unity:** Positive news stories often focus on acts of kindness, generosity, and community support. This fosters a sense of connection, shared humanity, and community resilience.

8 **Strengthens Social Bonds:** Uplifting stories help build a sense of trust and cooperation within communities, emphasizing the positive aspects of human relationships.

9 **Alters Perspectives:** Constant exposure to negative news can lead to a skewed perception of the world. Positive news stories provide a more balanced view, challenging negative stereotypes and biases.

10 **Encourages Empathy:** Uplifting stories that highlight human achievements and triumphs encourage empathy and understanding, fostering a more compassionate society.

11 **Positive Impact on Cognitive Functions:** Consuming positive news has been associated with enhanced cognitive functions, including improved problem-solving skills and creativity.

12 **Optimizes Brain Function:** Positive emotions triggered by uplifting stories contribute to the optimal functioning of the brain, promoting a positive mindset.

13 **Positive Reinforcement:** Positive news stories can serve as positive reinforcement in relationships, workplaces, and communities. They contribute to a culture of appreciation and gratitude.

14 **Reduces Conflict:** A focus on positive aspects of individuals and communities can contribute to reduced conflict and foster a more collaborative and supportive environment.

15 **Hopeful Outlook:** Positive news stories provide a sense of hope and optimism,

reinforcing the idea that positive change is possible.

Resources for Finding Constructive and Inspiring Content

Finding constructive and inspiring content can greatly contribute to personal development, motivation, and overall well-being. Here are various types of resources where you can discover such content:

1 **Self-help and Motivational Books:** Authors like David Humble, Tony Robbins, Brené Brown, and Simon Sinek often provide insightful and uplifting content.

2 **Biographies and Autobiographies:** Reading about the life journeys of successful and inspirational individuals

can be motivating.

3 **Personal Development Podcasts:** Podcasts like "The Tim Ferriss Show," "The School of Greatness," and "TED Talks Daily" feature interviews and discussions that can inspire personal growth.

4 **Storytelling Podcasts:** Shows like "The Moth" or "Snap Judgment" share real-life stories that can be both entertaining and thought-provoking.

5 **TED Talks:** The TED platform hosts talks on a wide range of topics, from science to motivation, providing valuable insights and inspiration.

6 **Medium:** A platform for writers to share their thoughts and experiences on

various subjects. You can find many articles on personal development and inspiration.

7 **Brain Pickings:** A blog by Maria Popova that explores a wide range of topics, including literature, science, and philosophy, often with a focus on meaningful and inspiring content.

8 **Goalcast:** A channel that shares motivational speeches and real-life success stories.

9 **Calm or Headspace:** These meditation apps not only help with relaxation but often include motivational content and life advice.

10 **Audible or Blinkist:** Audiobook platforms that offer summaries or full versions of

inspirational books.

11 **Instagram and Pinterest:** Follow accounts that share motivational quotes, success stories, and positive affirmations.

12 **LinkedIn:** Connect with thought leaders and influencers in your industry for inspiring professional content.

13 **Coursera, Udemy, or Khan Academy:** Platforms offering courses on personal development, mindfulness, and various skills.

14 **MasterClass:** Learn from experts in various fields, including business, writing, and art.

15 **Netflix or Amazon Prime:** Look for documentaries and films that showcase real stories of resilience, achievement,

and personal growth.

16 **Meetup or local clubs:** Joining local groups with shared interests can provide an opportunity to connect with inspiring individuals and share experiences.

Remember to curate your sources based on your personal interests

Chapter 6

The Social Impact

"The Social Impact" addresses the broader consequences of individuals' mental well-being on the collective social fabric.

In a digitally connected world, the constant exposure to negative news can contribute to a heightened sense of fear, polarization, and anxiety within communities.

By recognizing the interconnected nature of mental health and societal dynamics, "The Social Impact" emphasizes the importance of individuals adopting healthier news consumption habits as a means to foster more empathetic and cohesive societies.

The prescription acknowledges that the collective mental health of a community is intricately linked to the information environment, advocating for a mindful and intentional approach to news consumption that can positively influence social harmony.

In the context of "The News Detox Prescription," The Social Impact reinforces the idea that individual actions in managing news consumption ripple into the broader social landscape.

The prescription contends that by promoting mental well-being at an individual level, there is potential for a cascading effect that contributes to a more informed, understanding, and resilient society.

How our Individual News Consumption Habits Contribute to the Collective Social Mindset

Our individual news consumption habits play a significant role in shaping the collective social mindset.

The aggregation of individual perspectives, preferences, and reactions to news creates a shared narrative that influences societal attitudes, beliefs, and behaviors.

Here are several ways in which individual news consumption habits contribute to the collective social mindset:

1 **Individual Influence:** The news stories individuals choose to consume contribute to the formation of their values, beliefs, and worldviews.

   Collective Impact: As individuals with similar preferences gravitate towards certain types of news, shared values and beliefs emerge, influencing the collective social mindset.

2 **Individual Filter Bubbles:** Individuals often select news sources that align with their pre-existing beliefs and preferences, creating filter bubbles.

Collective Echo Chambers: When many individuals within a society engage in similar filtering behaviors, it reinforces existing biases and contributes to the creation of echo chambers where like-minded individuals reinforce each other's perspectives.

3 **Individual Conversations:** News topics that individuals find engaging or concerning become subjects of their conversations with friends, family, and colleagues.

Collective Discourse: Over time, these individual conversations contribute to a broader societal discourse, influencing how certain issues are perceived and discussed at a societal level.

4 **Individual Political Preferences:** News consumption habits influence individual political opinions and preferences.

Collective Political Landscape: Aggregated individual political perspectives shape the overall political landscape, influencing elections, policy debates, and public opinion on political issues.

5 **Individual Awareness:** News stories about social issues, cultural shifts, or scientific advancements contribute to individual awareness.

Collective Attitudes: The accumulation of individual awareness and reactions shapes collective attitudes and behaviors towards societal issues, influencing societal norms and values.

6 **Individual Perception:** How individuals perceive and interpret news about social challenges, such as climate change, inequality, or healthcare, affects their understanding of these issues.

Collective Response: Aggregated individual perceptions contribute to the collective response to social challenges, influencing societal priorities, activism, and the demand for change.

7 **Individual Cultural Preferences:** News consumption is influenced by cultural preferences, including preferences for news sources that align with cultural identities.

Collective Cultural Identity: The news stories that gain prominence within a cultural or social group contribute to the collective identity, influencing how that group is perceived and perceives itself.

8 **Individual Awareness of Issues:** News consumption informs individuals about societal issues, injustices, and opportunities for change.

Collective Civic Engagement: Aggregated individual awareness contributes to the collective level of civic engagement, activism, and social movements.

9 **Individual Trends:** Individual preferences for specific types of media, platforms, or formats shape media consumption trends.

Industry Response: Media outlets respond to these trends, reinforcing or adjusting their content to align with audience preferences, creating a feedback loop that influences the collective media landscape.

10 **Individual Interest in Educational Content:** News stories that individuals find educational or informative influence their interests in certain topics.

Collective Educational Priorities: Aggregated individual interests contribute to the prioritization of certain educational topics within society, influencing educational curricula and public discourse.

Chapter 8

News Literacy for the Modern Age

In an era where misinformation and sensationalism can permeate news cycles, fostering news literacy becomes essential for individuals seeking to navigate the media landscape responsibly.

This concept encourages individuals to develop the skills necessary to critically evaluate and discern the reliability of information sources.

With the rapid proliferation of news through various online platforms, understanding the mechanisms of news production, distribution, and the potential for bias becomes paramount.

By cultivating news literacy skills, individuals contribute to a media landscape where reliable information prevails, and the negative impact of sensationalized news is mitigated, aligning with the broader objectives of "The News Detox Prescription."

Promoting Media Literacy and Critical Thinking Skills

Promoting media literacy and critical thinking skills is crucial in today's rapidly evolving news landscape.

Media literacy includes skills such as identifying bias, recognizing different media genres, understanding the persuasive techniques used in media, and evaluating the credibility of sources.

Here are some important factors to consider in promoting media literacy and critical thinking:

1 **Questioning and Analyzing:** Question information, verify facts, and analyze sources. Critical thinking involves evaluating evidence, identifying logical fallacies, and recognizing when information is incomplete or misleading.

2 **Skepticism and Open-mindedness:** Promote a healthy level of skepticism while also fostering an open mind. Critical thinkers are willing to consider different perspectives and are open to changing their views based on evidence.

3 **Fact-Checking:** Learn how to fact-check information using reliable sources. Encourage the use of fact-checking websites and tools to verify claims before accepting them as true.

4 **Understanding Biases:** Recognize your own biases and understand the potential biases present in media sources. Acknowledge the impact of confirmation bias on your consumption of information.

5 **Online Source Evaluation:** Evaluate the credibility of online sources. Check for authorship, publication dates, and the overall reputation of the platform or website.

6 **Social Media Awareness:** Critically assess information shared on social media

platforms. Also, be cautious about misinformation that may spread rapidly through social networks.

The Responsibility of Consumers in Shaping a Healthier News Ecosystem.

Consumers play a crucial role in shaping a healthier news ecosystem.

As active participants in the information environment, their choices, behaviors, and demands influence the content produced, the credibility of news sources, and the overall dynamics of the media landscape.

Here are key responsibilities consumers have in contributing to a healthier news ecosystem:

1 **Verify Information:** Consumers should develop the habit of fact-checking information before accepting it as true. Verifying claims and cross-referencing information from multiple sources can help prevent the spread of misinformation.

2 **Question Biases:** Being aware of personal biases and questioning the potential biases in news sources is essential. Consumers should seek diverse perspectives and critically assess the framing of news stories.

3 **Avoid Echo Chambers:** Consumers should actively seek out information from a variety of sources, including those with

different perspectives.

Avoiding echo chambers helps prevent the reinforcement of pre-existing beliefs and promotes a more balanced understanding of issues.

4 **Support Quality Journalism:** Subscribing to reputable news outlets, whether local or international, helps sustain quality journalism.

Financial support from consumers is crucial for media organizations to continue producing reliable and investigative reporting.

5 **Invest in Learning:** Consumers should invest time in improving their media literacy skills.

Understanding the basics of how news is

produced, recognizing journalistic standards, and being familiar with common misinformation tactics are essential for making informed decisions.

6 **Teach Others:** Share media literacy knowledge with family, friends, and community members. By collectively promoting media literacy, consumers contribute to a more informed and discerning society.

7 **Verify Before Sharing:** Before sharing information on social media or other platforms, consumers should verify the accuracy of the content. This simple step can prevent the unintentional spread of misinformation.

8 **Use Reliable Sources:** Consumers should prioritize sharing information from reputable sources. Sharing content from credible news outlets contributes to a more reliable and trustworthy online

9 **Provide Feedback:** Consumers can actively engage with news outlets by providing constructive feedback. Encourage responsible reporting, fact-checking, and adherence to ethical standards. Constructive criticism helps media organizations improve their practices.

10 **Hold Media Accountable:** When news outlets fail to meet journalistic standards, consumers have the responsibility to hold them accountable.

This can be done through public discourse, social media discussions, or direct communication with the media organization.

11 **Support Public Accountability:** Consumers can support initiatives that advocate for transparency and accountability in media.

Public pressure and demand for ethical journalism can lead to positive changes in the news ecosystem.

12 **Participate in Media Literacy Initiatives:** Engage with and support initiatives that promote media literacy, both online and offline.

By participating in educational programs, consumers contribute to a more media-literate society.

13 **Avoid Clickbait and Sensationalism:** Consumers should be cautious of sensationalized headlines and clickbait. Supporting media outlets that prioritize accuracy over sensationalism encourages responsible journalism.

14 **Resist Polarization:** Consciously resist engaging in or supporting content that promotes extreme polarization. Encourage a more nuanced and balanced discourse on complex issues.

Cultivating Resilience

"Cultivating Resilience" stands as a guiding principle for navigating the challenges posed by a constant stream of negative news.

In the face of adversity, cultivating resilience involves developing the mental and emotional fortitude needed to withstand the impacts of distressing information while maintaining a sense of balance.

The prescription recognizes that frequent exposure to negative news can erode mental well-being, and cultivating resilience becomes a proactive strategy to build a psychological shield against the potential harm.

By fostering resilience, individuals are better equipped to absorb and process challenging information without succumbing to feelings of despair or helplessness.

This concept encourages individuals to adopt practices that enhance their ability to bounce back from the emotional toll of negative news, emphasizing the importance of self-care, mindfulness, and intentional news consumption.

By actively cultivating resilience, individuals not only protect their own mental well-being but also contribute to the broader goal of creating a society that can face challenges with strength and adaptability.

The prescription advocates for the integration of resilience-building practices into daily life, acknowledging their transformative potential in fostering a healthier mindset amidst the pervasive negativity in the media landscape.

Tools to Build Emotional Resilience in the Face of Negative News

Building emotional resilience in the face of negative news is essential for maintaining mental well-being and a positive outlook.

Here are several tools and strategies that can help you cultivate emotional resilience:

1 **Mindfulness and Meditation:** Mindfulness practices help individuals stay present, manage stress, and foster emotional awareness.

   How to Use: Incorporate daily mindfulness or meditation sessions to develop the skill of observing thoughts and emotions without becoming overwhelmed.

2 **Limiting News Consumption:** Setting boundaries on news intake prevents information overload and reduces exposure to negativity.

How to Use: Designate specific times for news consumption, and limit the duration to avoid continuous exposure.

3 **Seeking Positive News Sources:** Balancing negative news with positive stories helps maintain a more optimistic perspective.

How to Use: Intentionally seek out news sources that focus on positive and uplifting content to counterbalance the negative information.

4 **Maintaining Social Connections:** Building and maintaining strong social connections provides emotional support during challenging times.

How to Use: Reach out to friends, family, or support networks to share feelings and experiences, fostering a sense of community.

5 **Cognitive Restructuring:** Identifying and challenging negative thought patterns helps reshape one's perspective.

How to Use: Practice recognizing and reframing negative thoughts by focusing on alternative, more positive interpretations of events.

6 **Expressive Writing:** Writing about emotions and experiences can be therapeutic, helping to process and release negative feelings.

How to Use: Journaling or expressive writing allows individuals to reflect on their reactions to news and explore their emotions in a constructive way.

7 **Setting Realistic Expectations:** Realistic expectations prevent excessive worry and disappointment.

How to Use: Acknowledge that negative events occur, but also recognize that not every news story reflects the entire reality of a situation.

8 **Engaging in Physical Activity:** Regular exercise has positive effects on mental health, reducing stress and improving mood.

How to Use: Incorporate physical activity into the routine, whether it's walking, jogging, yoga, or any form of exercise that brings enjoyment.

9 **Practicing Self-Compassion:** Being kind to oneself in the face of challenges

fosters emotional resilience.

How to Use: Treat yourself with the same compassion you would offer a friend, acknowledging that it's okay to feel upset or overwhelmed by negative news.

10 **Staying Informed Without Dwelling:** Being informed is important, but dwelling on negative information can be detrimental.

How to Use: Stay informed about important issues without continuously revisiting distressing details. Balance awareness with intentional breaks from news consumption.

11 **Engaging in Hobbies and Leisure Activities:** Pursuing enjoyable activities promotes relaxation and provides a mental break from negative news.

How to Use: Dedicate time to hobbies, leisure activities, or interests that bring joy and a sense of accomplishment.

12 **Professional Support:** Seeking guidance from mental health professionals can provide additional tools for managing emotional challenges.

How to Use: If negative news significantly impacts mental well-being, consider consulting with a therapist or counselor for personalized strategies and support.

Encouraging a Proactive and Resilient Mindset

Encouraging a proactive and resilient mindset is crucial in navigating the challenges of the modern world, characterized by rapid changes, uncertainties, and complex problems.

Here are strategies to foster a proactive and resilient mindset:

1 **Embrace Challenges:** Cultivate a growth mindset by seeing challenges as opportunities for learning and personal development rather than insurmountable obstacles.

2 **Believe in Potential:** Recognize that abilities and intelligence can be developed through effort and learning.

3 **Create SMART Goals:** Establish specific, measurable, achievable, relevant, and time-bound goals to provide clear direction.

4 **Celebrate Progress:** Acknowledge and celebrate small achievements along the way, fostering a sense of accomplishment.

5 **Embrace Change:** Develop a mindset that welcomes change as a natural part of life. Seek opportunities for growth and learning in new situations.

6 **Learn from Failure:** View failures as opportunities to learn and adjust strategies, rather than as permanent setbacks.

7 **Self-awareness:** Understand and manage your own emotions effectively.

8 **Empathy:** Develop the ability to understand and connect with the emotions of others, fostering positive relationships.

9 **Present Moment Awareness:** Cultivate mindfulness to stay focused on the present moment and avoid excessive worry about the future.

10 **Stress Reduction:** Mindfulness practices, such as meditation and deep breathing, can help manage stress and enhance resilience.

11 **Identify Solutions:** Train yourself to approach challenges by focusing on potential solutions rather than dwelling

on problems.

12 **Seek Support:** Collaborate with others to brainstorm ideas and gain diverse perspectives on problem-solving.

13 **Build Connections:** Establish strong social connections with individuals who provide emotional support and encouragement.

14 **Open Communication:** Communicate openly about challenges, seeking advice and feedback from trusted friends, family, or mentors.

15 **Prioritize Tasks:** Learn to prioritize tasks based on importance and deadlines.

16 **Avoid Procrastination:** Break larger tasks into smaller, manageable steps to avoid feeling overwhelmed.

17 **Physical Well-Being:** Prioritize healthy habits, including regular exercise, proper nutrition, and sufficient sleep.

18 **Positive Reframing:** Train your mind to reframe negative thoughts into more positive or constructive perspectives.

19 **Learn from Setbacks:** Consider setbacks as opportunities for learning and growth rather than as failures.

20 **Stay Curious:** Cultivate a curious mindset by staying informed about new developments and actively seeking knowledge.

21 **Lifelong Learning:** Embrace a mindset of continuous learning to adapt to evolving challenges and opportunities.

22 **Take Responsibility:** Develop a sense of ownership and responsibility for your actions and decisions.

23 **Proactive Approach:** Be proactive in seeking opportunities and addressing challenges rather than waiting for things to happen.

24 **Reflect on Positives:** Regularly reflect on things you are grateful for, fostering a positive outlook.

25 **Appreciate Progress:** Acknowledge and appreciate personal and professional achievements.

26 **Adapt to Change:** Develop flexibility in your thinking and actions, adjusting plans when necessary.

27 **Be Open-minded:** Embrace different perspectives and be open to new ideas and approaches.

28 **Continuous Improvement:** Invest in your professional development to enhance skills and knowledge.

29 **Adapt to Career Changes:** Embrace opportunities for career growth and adapt to changes in the professional landscape.

Chapter 9

Steps to Achieve News Detox

News detox, or taking a break from consuming news, can be beneficial for mental health and overall well-being, especially in today's fast-paced and often overwhelming media landscape.

Here are some steps you can take to detox from news:

1 **Acknowledge the Need**: Recognize when you're feeling overwhelmed or you exhibit signs of news addiction as discussed in chapter 1.

If you find yourself constantly checking news apps or websites and feeling stressed, it might be time for a detox.

2 **Set Clear Goals**: Decide on the duration and extent of your news detox. It could be a complete break from all news sources for a certain period, or it could involve limiting your exposure to specific types of news (e.g., avoiding negative news, politics, etc.).

3 **Inform Others**: Let friends, family, and colleagues know that you'll be taking a break from news. This can help manage expectations and reduce pressure to stay updated on current events.

4 **Create Boundaries**: Set boundaries for when and how you consume news. Consider turning off news notifications on your devices, unsubscribing from

newsletters, and removing news apps from your phone.

5 **Find Alternative Activities**: Fill the time you would have spent consuming news with activities that promote relaxation and well-being.

This could include exercise, meditation, hobbies, spending time with loved ones, or engaging in creative pursuits.

6 **Curate Your Environment**: Surround yourself with positive influences during your news detox.

Seek out uplifting content such as books, podcasts, or movies that inspire or entertain you.

7 **Stay Informed Selectively**: If completely disconnecting from the news isn't

feasible or desirable, consider selectively choosing the sources and topics you engage with.

Focus on high-quality journalism and limit exposure to sensationalized or repetitive coverage.

8 **Practice Mindfulness**: Stay present and mindful of your thoughts and emotions during your news detox.

Notice how you feel when you're not constantly bombarded by news and pay attention to any changes in your mood or stress levels.

9 **Evaluate Your Experience**: After your news detox period, take some time to reflect on how you feel.

Notice any differences in your mood, stress levels, and overall well-being. Use this reflection to inform your future news consumption habits.

10 **Gradual Reintegration**: When you feel ready to reintroduce news into your life, do so gradually and intentionally.

Pay attention to how different sources and topics affect your mood and well-being, and adjust your consumption accordingly.

Remember that the goal of a news detox is not to remain uninformed but to cultivate a healthier relationship with news consumption. By taking regular breaks and being mindful of your media habits, you can better manage stress and maintain a balanced perspective on current events.

How to Stop Ruminating about Negative news

Rumination about negative news occurs when you repeatedly dwell on distressing information, replaying it in your mind without resolution. This can lead to heightened anxiety, stress, and a sense of helplessness.

Here's how to stop this cycle:

1 **Awareness:** Recognize when you're ruminating. Pay attention to your thought patterns and emotions, noticing when you're getting caught up in negative news cycles.

2 **Limit Exposure:** Reduce your intake of negative news. Set boundaries on how much time you spend consuming news media to prevent overexposure.

3 **Engage in Positive Distractions:** When you catch yourself ruminating, deliberately shift your focus to positive and uplifting activities. This could be anything from exercise to spending time with loved ones to pursuing hobbies.

4 **Challenge Negative Thoughts:** Question the accuracy and helpfulness of your rumination. Ask yourself if there's any action you can take in response to the news and whether worrying about it excessively serves any purpose.

5 **Practice Mindfulness:** Cultivate mindfulness techniques to help you stay present and grounded. Mindfulness meditation, deep breathing exercises, or simply focusing on your surroundings can interrupt the rumination cycle.

6 **Set Time Limits:** Allocate specific time periods for consuming news, and once that time is up, intentionally shift your attention to other things. This helps prevent continuous rumination throughout the day.

7 **Seek Support:** Talk to friends, family, or a therapist about your concerns. Sharing your thoughts and feelings with others can provide perspective and support.

8 **Take Action:** If there's something you can do to address the issue behind the negative news, take action. This could involve volunteering, donating to relevant causes, or engaging in advocacy work.

9 **Practice Self-Compassion:** Be kind to yourself and recognize that it's natural to feel overwhelmed by negative news at times. Treat yourself with the same empathy and understanding you would offer to a friend in distress.

Breaking the cycle of rumination takes time and effort, but with patience and persistence, you can learn to manage your response to negative news more effectively.

How to Quit Mindless Scrolling

Quitting mindless scrolling on social media can greatly improve your productivity, mental well-being, and overall quality of life. Here are some practical steps to help you break the habit:

1 **Set Specific Goals:** Define why you want to reduce mindless scrolling and set clear goals for yourself. Whether it's to reclaim lost time, improve focus, or prioritize real-life interactions, having a clear purpose will motivate you to stay on track.

2 **Track Your Usage:** Use built-in features on social media platforms or third-party apps to track how much time you spend scrolling each day. Seeing the actual time

spent can be eye-opening and serve as a reality check.

3 **Establish Boundaries:** Set specific times during the day when you allow yourself to use social media, and stick to them. Designate certain times as "social media-free zones" such as meal times, before bed, or during work hours.

4 **Remove Temptations:** Minimize the triggers that lead to mindless scrolling by removing social media apps from your phone's home screen or turning off notifications. Out of sight, out of mind.

5 **Find Alternatives:** Replace the habit of mindless scrolling with more productive or fulfilling activities. This could include reading a book, going for a walk,

practicing a hobby, or spending quality time with loved ones.

6 **Practice Mindfulness:** Be present and intentional when using social media. Before opening an app, ask yourself why you're doing it and what you hope to gain. Set a time limit for your session and stick to it.

7 **Curate Your Feed:** Unfollow accounts that don't add value to your life or contribute to mindless scrolling. Instead, follow accounts that inspire, educate, or entertain you in a meaningful way.

8 **Engage Purposefully:** When you do use social media, engage with intention rather than passively scrolling. Comment on posts, share meaningful content, and

connect with others in a meaningful way.

9 **Seek Support:** Share your goals with friends or family members and ask for their support in holding you accountable. Consider joining online communities or support groups focused on reducing social media usage.

10 **Be Patient and Persistent:** Breaking the habit of mindless scrolling takes time and effort. Be patient with yourself and celebrate small victories along the way. If you slip up, don't be discouraged; instead, learn from the experience and recommit to your goals.

Mindfulness as a Solution

Mindfulness is a mental state characterized by being fully present in the moment, acknowledging and accepting one's thoughts and feelings without judgment.

The practice of mindfulness has gained increasing recognition for its positive impact on cognitive functions, especially in the context of managing the effects of negativity.

Here are key points highlighting the importance of mindfulness and its impact on cognitive functions:

1 **Reducing Cognitive Distortions:** Mindfulness encourages individuals to observe their thoughts without

attachment or judgment.

This awareness helps to identify and reduce cognitive distortions, such as overgeneralization, catastrophizing, and black-and-white thinking, which are often associated with exposure to negative news.

2 **Enhancing Emotional Regulation:** Mindfulness practices, such as meditation and deep breathing, have been shown to enhance emotional regulation.

This is crucial in dealing with the emotional impact of negative news and preventing it from overwhelming cognitive functions.

3 **Improving Attention and Concentration:** Regular mindfulness practice has been

linked to improvements in attention and concentration.

By training the mind to focus on the present moment, individuals can reduce the cognitive impact of constant exposure to negative information.

4 **Mitigating the Impact of Stress:** Mindfulness-based interventions have proven effective in reducing stress and the physiological responses associated with it.

Chronic exposure to negative news can induce stress, and mindfulness helps mitigate its impact on cognitive functions by promoting relaxation and a more balanced mental state.

5 **Preventing Rumination:** Negative news can lead to rumination, where individuals repetitively dwell on negative thoughts. Mindfulness disrupts this pattern by redirecting attention to the present moment, preventing the prolonged engagement with negative content that can otherwise impair cognitive functions.

6 **Enhancing Cognitive Flexibility:** Mindfulness has been associated with improved cognitive flexibility, the ability to adapt thinking to different situations. This can be valuable in processing negative information more objectively and developing a more balanced perspective.

7 **Promoting Non-reactivity:** Mindfulness fosters non-reactivity, encouraging individuals to respond to stimuli, including negative news, with intention rather than impulsivity.

This measured response can prevent the automatic and often exaggerated cognitive reactions to negative information.

8 **Encouraging Positive Neuroplasticity:** Regular mindfulness practice has been linked to positive changes in the brain's structure and function.

This includes promoting neuroplasticity, the brain's ability to adapt and reorganize itself. This can potentially counteract the negative impact of persistent exposure to distressing news.

Here are some examples of meditation activities which you can practice when you feel overwhelmed:

1 **Breath Awareness Meditation**: Find a quiet and comfortable space to sit or lie down. Close your eyes and bring your attention to your breath.

Notice the sensation of each inhale and exhale as you breathe naturally. When your mind starts to wander, gently guide your focus back to your breath.

You can use a specific anchor point, such as the rise and fall of your abdomen or the feeling of air passing through your nostrils, to help maintain your concentration.

2 **Body Scan Meditation**: Lie down in a comfortable position and close your eyes. Starting from your toes, bring your awareness to each part of your body sequentially, slowly scanning up to your head.

Notice any sensations, tensions, or areas of relaxation as you move through each body part. Take your time and allow yourself to fully experience the present moment without judgment.

3 **Loving-Kindness Meditation**: Sit comfortably with your eyes closed. Begin by directing loving-kindness towards yourself, silently repeating phrases such as "May I be happy, may I be healthy, may I be safe, may I live with ease."

Then, extend these wishes outward to others, starting with those affected by the negative news you've just heard or read about, then to your friends, and eventually to all beings.

Visualize each person or group as you repeat the phrases, cultivating feelings of compassion and goodwill.

4 **Guided Visualization Meditation**: Listen to a guided meditation recording or follow a script that leads you through a visualization journey.

This could involve imagining a peaceful place in nature, visualizing yourself accomplishing a goal, or envisioning a state of deep relaxation and healing.

Allow yourself to immerse in the imagery and sensations invoked by the guided instructions.

5 **Walking Meditation:** Find a quiet outdoor space or walk in a slow, deliberate manner indoors.

Pay attention to each step you take, feeling the sensation of your feet making contact with the ground.

Notice the movement of your body and the surrounding environment as you walk.

If your mind wanders, gently bring your focus back to the physical sensations of walking.

6 **Mantra Meditation:** Choose a word, phrase, or sound that holds personal

significance or resonates with you spiritually.

Repeat this mantra silently or aloud as you meditate, allowing it to become a focal point for your attention. Let the mantra anchor your mind and bring you into a state of deep relaxation and inner peace.

These meditation activities can be adapted to suit your preferences and needs, providing valuable opportunities to cultivate mindfulness, reduce stress, and enhance overall well-being. Experiment with different techniques to discover which ones resonate most with you.

Conclusion

As we reach the culmination of "The News Detox Prescription: Restoring Health in a World of Negativity," it is my sincere hope that you have found not only insights into the impact of news consumption on your well-being but also practical tools to navigate the information landscape with mindfulness and intentionality.

In our journey together, we've explored the overwhelming influence of negativity, the weight it places on our minds, and the toll it takes on our overall health.

We've uncovered the power of conscious media consumption, emphasizing the importance of quality over quantity in the news we choose to engage with.

Through mindfulness exercises and the cultivation of discernment, we've laid the groundwork for a healthier relationship with the information that surrounds us.

Remember, this journey is not about tuning out the world but rather tuning into a more balanced and positive perspective.

It's about recognizing the agency you hold in shaping your mental and emotional landscape, even in the face of challenging global events.

By embracing the principles outlined in this prescription, you empower yourself to be a conscious consumer of news, fostering resilience, empathy, and a sense of agency.

As you embark on the path ahead, continue to prioritize your mental and emotional well-being. Integrate the lessons learned here into your daily life, and be mindful of the news you consume.

Seek out stories that inspire, uplift, and remind you of the inherent goodness in the world. Share these stories, creating ripples of positivity that contribute to a collective shift toward a healthier media ecosystem.

"The News Detox Prescription" is a guide for reclaiming your peace of mind and fostering a more positive and resilient outlook on life.

May the principles within these pages serve as a foundation for a future where we engage with the news not as passive recipients but as conscious contributors to a world that is both informed and inspired.

As you navigate the ever-changing currents of information, may you find balance, joy, and a renewed sense of purpose.

Wishing you a future filled with clarity, compassion, and a steadfast commitment to your well-being in a world of news.

www.ingramcontent.com/pod-product-compliance
Lightning Source LLC
Chambersburg PA
CBHW050822260726
48660CB00004B/1569